Momma Said!

By
Mariah S. Buchanan

Lessons to Live by:

ISBN: Softcover   978-1-9845-3432-3
        Hardcover   978-1-9845-3433-0
        EBook   978-1-9845-3431-6

Print information available on the last page

Rev. date: 08/06/2018

To order additional copies of this book, contact:
Xlibris
1-888-795-4274
www.Xlibris.com
Orders@Xlibris.com

Introduction

Growing up in the south with several sisters and brothers, our mom would have talks with us kids motivating us to become good citizens and also to teach family values. Our father passed away when I was very young and mom was left with being both parents. The difference in parents today and parents when I was young is that many parents now don't have or make time to do a lot of value teaching. I know I am lumping today's parents together; however, I am going on what I have surmised from teaching and watching the interaction of kids with adults and each other.

This book gives a sampling of the saying my mom used to tell us; some of them funny and some goes straight to the point. Each of them was something to live by. As kids we learned early how to respect what adults told us and to realize that learning came in many ways.

I hope you enjoy the many phases and pictures which were inspired by my mom and her mother. In hopes that what was taught to us as kids, will inspire you to keep them with you to share and maybe add your own to grow by.

The more you give the more you have to give!

You just wait until your
daddy comes home!

Some people talk with wooden
heads and paper tongues!

The Early Bird Catches the Worm!

A disobedient child has no good luck!

Choose your friends well!

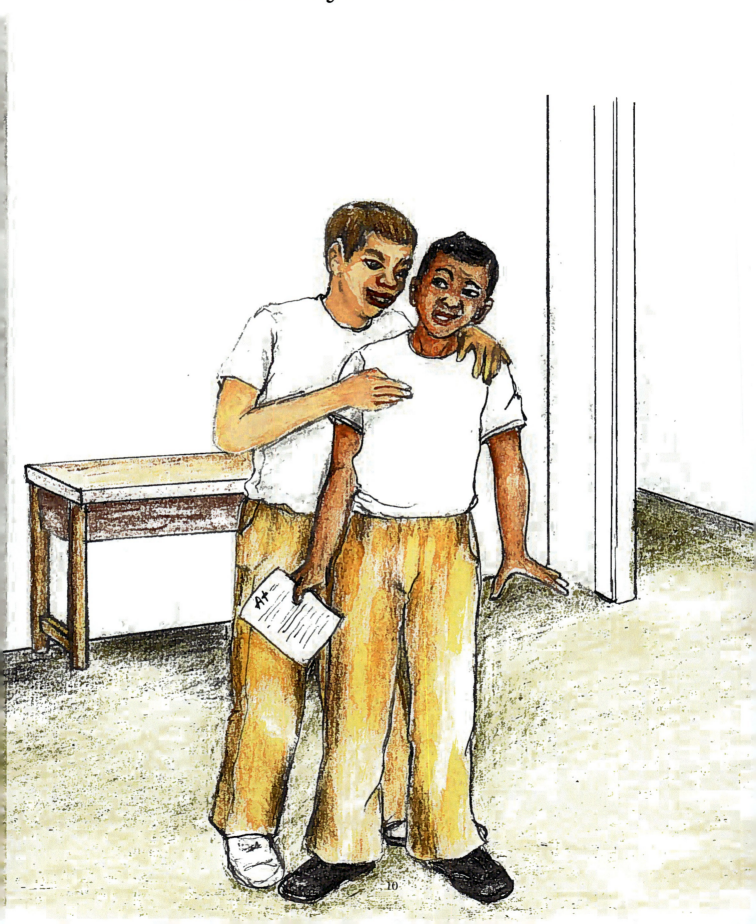

Practice makes perfect!

He who has a thousand friends, has not a friend to spare, but he who has one enemy will find him everywhere!

All that Glitters, is not Gold!

Give with an open hand!

Learn to love not hate!

Always keep a smile in your heart!

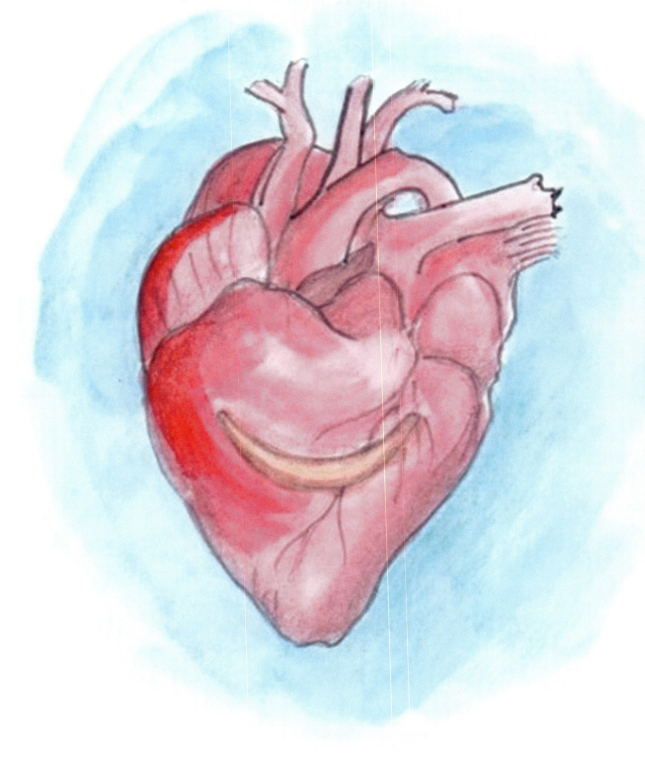

Don't build a stumbling block for others because you may trip over it!

A hard head makes a soft behind!

Don't let the sundown beat you home!

Mother knows best!

Have respect for yourself, and others will too!

Keep your dress down!

Everybody's not your friend!

Self pride is contagious.

Charity starts at home and spreads abroad!

Your word is your bond.

Don't take wooden nickels.

Finish what you start.

Glossary

1. The more you give, the more you have to give!

    When you are a giving person, you will receive with giving. You should tithe your time, money, and caring.

2. You just wait until your daddy comes home!

    Sometimes mothers allow the fathers to be the enforcers in the family.

3. Some people talk with wooden heads and paper tongues!

    Sometimes people speak nonsense, mostly saying a lot but meaning nothing.

4. The early bird catches the worm!

    Make plans to go to bed at a decent time and you can wake up refreshed in order to get an early start.

5. A disobedient child has no good luck!

    When you are constantly breaking the rules, you will always be in trouble.

6. Choose your friends well!

    Don't just think you can be friends with everyone. Some people may want to use you.

7. Practice makes perfect!

    Make sure you set regular practice time for things you want to be good or better at.

8. He who has a thousand friends, has not a friend to spare, but he who has one enemy will find him everywhere!

    You can be your own worst enemy.

9. All that glitters is not gold!

    Just because somethings looks priceless might be bad or bad for you.

10. Give with an open hand!

    When you give, give freely. Don't expect something in return.

11. Learn to love, not hate!

    When you talk to and get to know someone of another background, you will find out that you have a lot in common.

12. Always keep a smile in your heart!

    Try to keep a positive attitude in life.

13. Don't build a stumbling block for others, because you may trip over it!

    When you try to set someone else up, you are possibly setting yourself up for the same thing.

14. A hard head makes a soft behind!

    Many times when you don't follow the rules, you get punished. You might not be able to stand the punishment.

15. Don't let sundown beat you home!

    Young people should get in before it gets late. Being out in the streets is not a place to hang-out.

16. Mother knows best!

    Your mother has lived where you are trying to go, so listen.

17. Have respect for yourself and others will too!
    When you come out in public, you should remember that you bring what you learn from home with you. Consider what you wear and how you behave and look in public.
18. Keep your dress down!
    Young ladies should respect themselves by not being so fast to become a grown-up.
19. Everybody's not your friend!
    Some people may smile in your face and have bad motives – So give go slowly in making close friends.
20. Self-pride is contagious!
    Have pride in what you do and your surroundings.
21. Charity starts at home and spreads abroad!
    When you can give at home, sharing will spread far.
22. Your word is your bond!
    What you say should be said with importance and have meaning.
23. Don't take wooden nickels!
    Know when someone is not giving you the truth. Don't be so gullible.
24. Finish what you start!
    When you have a task, make sure you do your best to complete it.

Printed in the United States
By Bookmasters